EXPLORING
ANCIENT CITIES

EXCAVATION
EXPLORATION

JESSIE ALKIRE

**Checkerboard
Library**

An Imprint of Abdo Publishing
abdopublishing.com

abdopublishing.com

Published by Abdo Publishing, a division of ABDO, PO Box 398166, Minneapolis, Minnesota 55439. Copyright © 2019 by Abdo Consulting Group, Inc. International copyrights reserved in all countries. No part of this book may be reproduced in any form without written permission from the publisher. Checkerboard Library™ is a trademark and logo of Abdo Publishing.

Printed in the United States of America, North Mankato, Minnesota
052018
092018

THIS BOOK CONTAINS
RECYCLED MATERIALS

Design: Sarah DeYoung, Mighty Media, Inc.
Production: Mighty Media, Inc.
Editor: Megan Borgert-Spaniol
Design elements: Mighty Media, Inc., Shutterstock, Spoon Graphics
Cover photographs: Shutterstock, Spoon Graphics
Interior photographs: Alamy, p. 16; iStockphoto, pp. 8 (left, right), 11; Shutterstock, pp. 4, 5 (all), 7, 9 (top left, right), 13, 19, 21, 22 (bottom left), 25, 26, 29; Wikimedia Commons, pp. 9 (bottom left), 22 (top left, bottom right)

Library of Congress Control Number: 2017961545

Publisher's Cataloging-in-Publication Data
Names: Alkire, Jessie, author.
Title: Exploring ancient cities / by Jessie Alkire.
Description: Minneapolis, Minnesota : Abdo Publishing, 2019. I Series: Excavation
    exploration I Includes online resources and index.
Identifiers: ISBN 9781532115257 (lib.bdg.) I ISBN 9781532155970 (ebook)
Subjects: LCSH: Anthropology--Juvenile literature. I Cities and towns, ancient--Juvenile
    literature. I Discovery and exploration--Juvenile literature. I Excavations
    (Archaeology)--Juvenile literature.
Classification: DDC 930--dc23

CONTENTS

CLIMBING
THE MOUNTAIN

YOU LOOK UP AT THE TOWERING MOUNTAIN ABOVE.

Ahead of you, your guide shows no fear. You swallow your own fear and follow her on foot.

Rain and snow batter your face as you labor up the mountain. Your boots slip as you grab the rock face to steady yourself. You've been exploring South America for the past few years. You've been looking for lost cities. But your travels have not prepared you for this slippery mountain **trek**!

You know the danger will be worth it. As you ascend the mountain, your fear turns to excitement. Your guide shouts from ahead that you're close. You lift yourself up over a rocky ledge. And your mouth drops open.

In front of you is the most beautiful sight you've ever seen. A large settlement of stone buildings and pyramids lies before you. The buildings are dotted with plant growth and **rubble**. But they are perfectly preserved. Your heart soars at the thought of the **artifacts** and treasures waiting for you. What city is this? You step forward, shovel in hand, to find out!

WHAT ARE
ANCIENT CITIES?

Ancient cities are cities from hundreds or even thousands of years ago. These cities were **inhabited** by ancient civilizations, such as the Romans and Incas. Many of these cities were abandoned or destroyed centuries ago.

Ancient cities existed all over the world in many periods of history. But most cities had a few things in common. Their buildings often surrounded a central religious structure, such as a temple. Cities usually had government and laws. They also had markets where people sold goods. Some ancient cities, such as Troy, were surrounded by walls.

Archaeologists have studied ancient cities for hundreds of years. This practice began as a quest to find treasures and art. But it became a science in the 1700s and 1800s. Archaeologists excavate **artifacts**, skeletons, and more from ancient cities. They learn about the people who lived in the cities. They also learn about ancient cities' **architecture**, **culture**, and more!

Walls protected ancient cities against possible attacks by people from other cities. The walls of Troy were built with mud bricks and limestone blocks.

TIMELINE

1748

Excavations begin at Pompeii, a famous ancient city in Italy.

1870

Heinrich Schliemann begins excavations at Hisarlik in Turkey. He believes it is the site of the legendary city of Troy.

1860s

Excavations at Pompeii become more organized under archaeologist Giuseppe Fiorelli.

1885

Edward Herbert Thompson begins to investigate Chichén Itzá in Mexico.

1893–1894

Wilhelm Dörpfeld identifies and labels the different layers of Troy.

2012

Lidar **technology** helps archaeologists discover several ancient cities in the forests of Cambodia.

1911

Hiram Bingham discovers a lost Inca city at Machu Picchu in Peru's Andes Mountains.

2017

Researchers begin the first large investigation of Chichén Itzá in 50 years.

UNCOVERING ASHES

One of the most famous ancient cities is Pompeii. Pompeii is in Campania, Italy. The area was first settled in the 700s BCE. Pompeii grew into a large, lively city of about 20,000 people.

But Pompeii was located near a powerful volcano, Mount Vesuvius. The volcano erupted in 79 CE. Pompeii was buried under millions of tons of ash. About 2,000 **inhabitants** were killed!

Pompeii wasn't excavated until 1748. Explorers were looking for **artifacts** for the King of Naples, Charles III. The excavators dug through more than 20 feet (6 m) of ash and stone. The ash had preserved the city and everything in it.

The explorers excavated **intact** buildings and household

DIG THIS!

Pompeii was first identified in 1763. Workers found an **inscription** that read *Rei publicae Pompeianorum.* This means "the commonwealth of the Pompeians" in Latin.

Ash from Mount Vesuvius mixed with rain after the eruption. This formed a concrete-like mixture that preserved Pompeii.

items. Even skeletons were perfectly preserved. They showed how families fled or huddled in fear in the final moments of their lives.

Early excavations of Pompeii were not done in an organized manner. Excavators were mainly seeking treasures to display or sell. They weren't interested in studying the **artifacts** scientifically. Because of this, many historic artifacts were lost or damaged.

Excavations at Pompeii became more organized under archaeologist Giuseppe Fiorelli in the 1860s. Fiorelli divided Pompeii into nine regions. He assigned numbers to buildings to help researchers locate them. He also excavated houses from the top down. This helped to better preserve the buildings. These practices helped archaeology become scientific and systematic.

Fiorelli also developed a method to make casts of bodies. Bodies had left impressions in ash. Fiorelli poured plaster into these spaces. The plaster hardened into **replicas** of the bodies. These casts showed details of clothing, facial expressions, and more. Archaeologists learned what the people of Pompeii looked like and how they dressed.

Pompeii is still being excavated today. The city has taught archaeologists how ancient Romans built their cities and furnished their homes. Pompeii excavations have also taught archaeologists

DIG THIS!

Excavations have revealed what people ate in Pompeii. Archaeologists have uncovered perfectly preserved loaves of bread at the site. They have also found jars of fruit!

about social, economic, and religious life at the time. Sculptures, wall paintings, and other Pompeii **artifacts** have even inspired artists throughout history. These artifacts are still considered some of the finest examples of Roman art!

Archaeologists have uncovered many clay pots at Pompeii. Romans used these pots to store food and wine.

DIGGING
THROUGH LAYERS

Several hundred miles east of Pompeii is another buried city called Troy. Troy is located in what is now Turkey, on a mound called Hisarlik. The city was likely founded around 3000 BCE. But it was destroyed at least nine times throughout history. Each time, different groups of people built new cities on top of the old ones. This created a mound that was 105 feet (32 m) high!

The final Troy was abandoned by 1350 CE. Most people learned of Troy from literary works about the Trojan War. This legendary war was said to be fought by ancient Greeks against the citizens of Troy. But English scholar Frank Calvert believed Troy was real. He determined Hisarlik was the likely location of Troy.

Calvert began to explore Hisarlik in 1860. But he didn't have enough money to conduct full excavations. He convinced German archaeologist Heinrich Schliemann to take over the work. Schliemann was a wealthy businessman. He hired a team of 150 laborers. Schliemann and his team began excavations in 1870.

LAYERS OF TROY

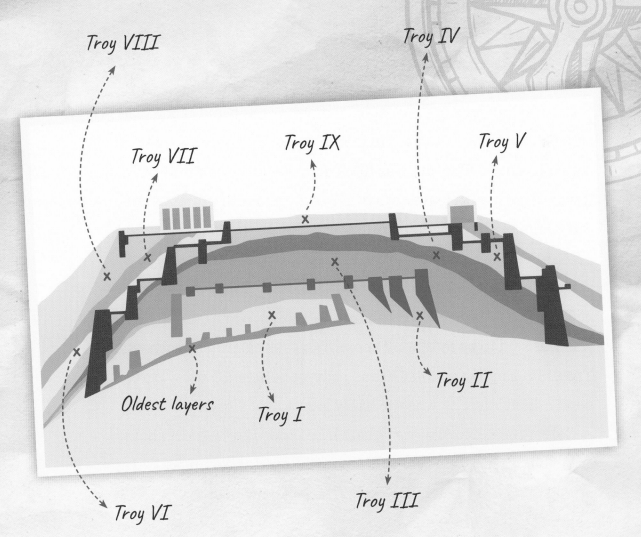

Troy VIII

Troy IV

Troy VII

Troy IX

Troy V

Oldest layers

Troy I

Troy II

Troy VI

Troy III

Archaeologists have found evidence that suggests most layers of Troy were destroyed by earthquake or fire.

Schliemann's team dug trenches to the bottom of the mound. They used shovels, wheelbarrows, and horse-drawn carts to remove tons of earth and **rubble**. In the process, Schliemann destroyed some of the upper layers of the city. But Schliemann also unearthed **artifacts** such as bracelets, rings, and other jewelry.

Other archaeologists took over excavations after Schliemann. In 1893 and 1894, German Wilhelm Dörpfeld continued identifying and labeling the different layers of Troy. In the 1930s, American Carl Blegen helped date different areas of the site.

Archaeologists have also sought proof that the Trojan War occurred. Blegen discovered that Troy VII had arrowheads in the walls. It also had bodies laid in the streets and other signs of war. Such evidence suggests a war or wars did occur at Troy.

Troy's discovery made archaeologists more interested in prehistoric sites. It taught them the importance of excavating carefully and dating artifacts. Troy also showed that real events may have inspired the myth of the Trojan War!

UNDERWATER
EXCAVATIONS

Not all ancient cities were buried or destroyed. Chichén Itzá is one such city. It is located on the Yucatán **Peninsula** in Mexico. The city was founded in the 500s CE by the Maya people.

Chichén Itzá was abandoned around 1500 CE. But it was not until the mid-1800s that explorers began to excavate the city. In 1885, American archaeologist Edward Herbert Thompson started investigating the ruins.

Thompson became interested in a sacred **sinkhole** on the site called a cenote. The cenote was about 80 feet (24 m) deep and filled with water. Thompson hoped to find **artifacts** at the bottom of the cenote. He used a crane to lower a scoop into the water and then bring it back up. He also used a diving suit and air tanks to dive into the cenote!

Thompson found incense, vases, and skeletons in the cenote. He determined that religious **rituals** took place there. People and

Chichén Itzá is also known for its pyramid, El Castillo. It has 365 steps, one for each day of the year!

objects were likely thrown into the cenote as sacrifices to the Maya rain god, Chaac.

Thompson's cenote exploration taught archaeologists about Maya beliefs and traditions. It also showed that underwater excavations could yield important Maya **artifacts**. Today, cenote exploration is a common archaeological practice in Maya regions.

LOST CITY
IN THE MOUNTAINS

Machu Picchu is a more recently founded ancient city. The Inca site is located in southern Peru. It was likely founded in 1450 CE. But no one knows what the site was used for. Some historians believe it was a royal estate. Others believe it was a religious center or military fortress.

Historians guess Machu Picchu was abandoned about a century after its construction. No written record of the city has been discovered. Some local people knew of its existence. But the first person to publicly note the city's importance was American archaeologist Hiram Bingham.

Bingham traveled to Peru in 1911 on an archaeological expedition. Local people spoke of ruins at the top of a mountain. Bingham traveled up the mountain. He was shocked by what he found.

Stone buildings, walls, and terraces rose from the earth at Machu Picchu. They had been untouched for 400 years. Plant growth covered the ruins. This had helped preserve the structures.

Machu Picchu is located in the Andes Mountains.
The site stands 7,970 feet (2,430 m) above sea level!

HIRAM BINGHAM

Hiram Bingham was an American archaeologist. He was also a skilled mountaineer. Bingham began exploring South America in 1906. In 1911, he found the world-famous ruins of Machu Picchu. He led excavations there the next year.

Bingham was also a history professor and politician. He went on to become a US senator in 1924. But Bingham remains most famous for sharing the wonders of Machu Picchu!

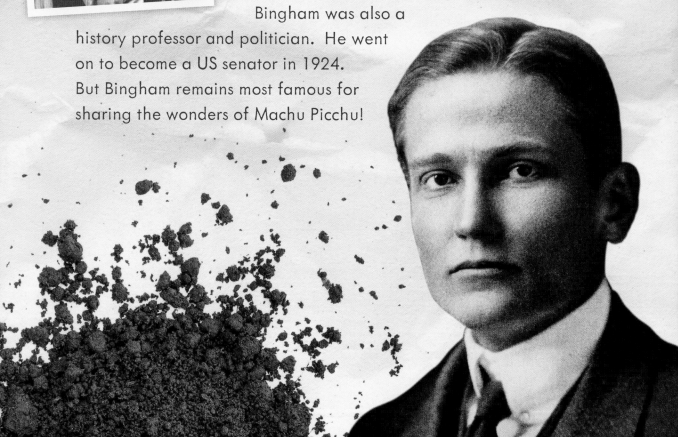

Bingham excavated thousands of **artifacts** from Machu Picchu. These included art, jewelry, knives, and axes. He also found skeletons.

These discoveries have taught archaeologists about Inca life. Researchers have also traced Machu Picchu artifacts to many different regions. This suggests that other groups besides the Inca may have lived in this ancient city.

Machu Picchu has also revealed much about Inca **architecture**. The site is made up of about 200 structures. The Inca did not use cement to build their structures. Instead, they cut granite pieces so they fit together perfectly. The buildings stood strong against weather and other forces.

The Inca also created a remarkable drainage system. They used layers of soil, dirt, gravel, and stones to filter rainwater. This kept the terraces from flooding. Such marvels showed archaeologists how the Inca made use of their natural landscape.

ANCIENT
CITIES & TECHNOLOGY

Excavations are still taking place at some of the world's famous ancient cities. And archaeologists continue to discover more ancient cities. Today, researchers use advanced tools to locate and map these hidden sites.

One **technology** is called Light Detecting and Ranging, or *lidar*. This system uses **lasers** to measure distance. Lidar measures the time it takes for a laser to bounce off an object and return to the device.

Lidar is often mounted on planes or helicopters. Its lasers scan the ground below. Archaeologists use lidar data to map a site's **topography**. The lasers can even see through thick plant growth. This is especially helpful in mapping tropical areas.

In 2012, researchers began using lidar to map miles of thick forest in Cambodia. They discovered several ancient cities buried below the forest floor. Archaeologists think lidar will help them learn much about mysterious tropical civilizations.

Archaeologists have surveyed miles of land around Cambodia's city of Angkor. The area is famous for its many temple ruins.

Experts estimate that 3,000 cenotes remain hidden beneath the forest of Chichén Itzá.

Lidar is also used to make new discoveries in cities that have already been excavated. Chichén Itzá is one of the latest sites to launch new excavations. In 2017, researchers began the first large investigation at Chichén Itzá in 50 years. They

DIG THIS!

Lidar was first used in the 1970s for space exploration. It was used to map the surface of the moon during the Apollo 15 mission!

planned to use lidar and heat sensors to find more hidden cenotes in the forest. Researchers hoped these **technologies** would allow for new discoveries without harming the site.

Researchers at Chichén Itzá also planned to use **3-D** imaging tools. These tools would create models of pyramids and other structures. Researchers could use this data to create 3-D maps of Chichén Itzá. Technologies like these will help archaeologists make new discoveries and learn more about ancient **cultures**.

FUTURE OF
ANCIENT CITIES

Ancient cities provide valuable glimpses of life in the past. But many of these sites have been damaged or **looted**. This is especially common at famous ancient cities that attract tourists.

Researchers are looking for solutions to these problems. At Machu Picchu, archaeologists use **drones** to both map the site and look for signs of damage. Researchers are also exploring virtual reality (VR) to protect ancient cities.

VR uses **3-D** images to create virtual ancient cities. People can use VR to experience the cities without physically being in them. Meanwhile, the real cities will receive less traffic and damage by visitors.

Archaeologists believe humans today can learn from ancient cities and their history. For example, ancient wars were similar to those fought today. We can use knowledge of ancient wars to handle or avoid present conflicts. As archaeologists explore the past, they help us to better understand the present!

VR companies such as California-based Jaunt allow users to virtually explore ancient cities such as Machu Picchu.

GLOSSARY

architecture — the art of planning and designing buildings.

artifact — an object made by humans long ago for a practical purpose.

culture — the customs, arts, and tools of a nation or a people at a certain time.

drone — an aircraft or ship that is controlled by radio signals.

inhabit — to live in or occupy a place. A person who inhabits a place is called an inhabitant.

inscription — something written or engraved on a surface.

intact — not broken or damaged.

laser — a device that creates a narrow beam of light.

loot — to steal things from a place, especially after a war or natural disaster.

peninsula — land that sticks out into water and is connected to a larger landmass.

replica — an exact copy.

ritual — a set form or order to a ceremony.

rubble — the rough, broken stones or bricks that are left after a building falls down.

sinkhole — a hole or sunken part of the ground caused by water erosion.

technology (tehk-NAH-luh-jee) — a machine or piece of equipment created using science and engineering, and made to do certain tasks.

3-D — having length, width, and height. "3-D" stands for *three-dimensional*.

topography — the shape, height, and depth of the features of a place. A topographic map indicates these features.

trek — a difficult journey.

ONLINE RESOURCES

Booklinks
NONFICTION
NETWORK
FREE! ONLINE NONFICTION RESOURCES

To learn more about ancient cities, visit **abdobooklinks.com**. These links are routinely monitored and updated to provide the most current information available.

INDEX